Accelerated Reader

Book Level 1.2 AR Pts 0.5

Rookie reader

Aggie and Will

By Larry Dane Brimner

Illustrated by Rebecca McKillip Thornburgh

Children's Press ®
A Division of Grolier Publishing
New York London Hong Kong Sydney
Danbury, Connecticut

For Helen Galvin
—L. D. B.

For Blair and Alice, obviously
—R. McK. T.

Reading Consultant
Linda Cornwell
Learning Resource Consultant
Indiana Department of Education

Visit Children's Press® on the Internet at:
http://publishing.grolier.com

Library of Congress Cataloging-in-Publication Data
Brimner, Larry Dane.
    Aggie and Will / by Larry Dane Brimner ; illustrated by Rebecca McKillip Thornbu
    p. cm. — (Rookie reader)
    Summary: Although Aggie and Will often disagree, they can still be friends.
    ISBN 0-516-20754-7 (lib. bdg.)   0-516-26409-5 (pbk.)
    [1. Friendship—Fiction.] I. Thornburgh, Rebecca McKillip, ill. II. Title. III. Series.
PZ7.B767Ag 1998
[E]—dc21   97-40054
                                                CIP
                                                AC

Aggie and Will never agree.

When Aggie wants ice cream,

Will wants cake.

Nifty
BAKING
TRICKS
by Alice

BAKIN
POWDE

CIRCUS CAKE

MAGIC FROSTING

When Aggie wants
to climb a tree,

8

Will wants to skate.

When Aggie wants to be alone,

Will wants her company.

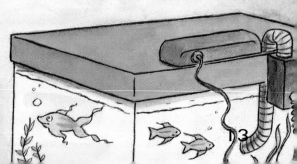

13

And when Will wants to be alone,

14

Aggie wants his company.

Aggie says,

16

"I am taller than a table."

Will says, "You are shorter
than a streetlight."

19

Will says,

"I jump higher than a frog."

Aggie says, "You jump lower
than that kite."

Who is right?

Don't ask Aggie.

Don't ask Will.

Aggie and Will never agree.

Well—almost never.

When Aggie wants
to go to the library,

so does Will.

About the Author

Larry Dane Brimner writes on a wide range of topics, from picture book and middle-grade fiction to young adult nonfiction. He has written many Rookie Readers, including *Lightning Liz, Dinosaurs Dance, Nana's Hog,* and *What Good Is a Tree?* Mr.

Brimner is also the author of *E-mail* and *The World Wide Web* for Children's Press and the award-winning *Merry Christmas, Old Armadillo* (Boyds Mills Press). He lives in the southwest region of the United States.

About the Illustrator

When she was growing up in Hollidaysburg, Pennsylvania, Rebecca McKillip Thornburgh had a race with her sister to see who could read every single book in the library. Now that she's more or less grown up, Rebecca still spends most of her time reading, but she also likes to draw pictures and eat cookies. Rebecca lives with her husband David and young daughters Blair and Alice in a pleasantly spooky old house in Philadelphia.